Women in PRISON

MINISTRY HANDBOOK

Sunny M. Lockwood

A Joint Project of
General Conference Ministerial Association
and
La Sierra University Women's Resource Center

Grateful acknowledgment to J. A. Thomas and Associates, Inc., Atlanta Georgia, for providing development costs for this book.

This handbook is a joint project of the following organizations:

General Conference Ministerial Association
12501 Old Columbia Pike
Silver Spring, MD 20904

Women's Resource Center
La Sierra University
4700 Pierce Street
Riverside, CA 92515

Editors: Kit Watts and Penny Shell

Proofreaders: Jocey Fay and Beverly Rumble

Date of Publication: June 2000

Bible Texts from the New Revised Standard Version

The model on the cover was photographed in a studio for illustrative purposes only.

Printed in Canada

Maracle Press
Oshawa, Ontario

ISBN 1-57847-068-4

Table of Contents

Section 2: Choosing Your Emphasis

Chapter Three

Chapter Four

SECTION I:

Getting the Picture

Introduction

You Can Make a Difference

How this book can help you

Perhaps you picked up this book because you are involved in a ministry to women in prison and are looking for new ideas and resources. Perhaps you know someone interested in prison ministries with whom to share it. Perhaps you have been considering such a ministry and want to know what it involves. Or perhaps it is the very beginning of your call to this special ministry.

Whatever your reason for looking in these pages, you will find a new understanding of the ministry of visiting those in prison, a ministry especially commended by Jesus:

> When the Son of man comes in his glory and all the angels with him, then he will sit on his throne of his glory. All the nations will be gathered before him, and he will separate people one from another as a shepherd separates the sheep from the goats, and he will put the sheep at his right hand and the goats at the left. Then the king will say to those at his right hand, "Come, you that are blessed by my Father, inherit the kingdom prepared for you from the foundation of the world; for I was hungry and you gave me food, I was thirsty and you gave me something to drink, I was a stranger and you welcomed me, I was naked and you gave me clothing, I was sick and you took care of me, I was in prison and you visited me."

> Then the righteous will answer him, "Lord, when was it that we saw you hungry and gave you food, or thirsty and gave you something to drink? And when was it that we saw you a stranger and welcomed you, or naked and gave you clothing? And when was it that we saw you sick or in prison and visited you?"
>
> And the king will answer them, "Truly I tell you, just as you did it to one of my least of these who are members of my family, you did to me." —Matthew 25:31-40[1]

Feeding the hungry, visiting the sick, and clothing the naked may seem easier than ministering to prisoners, yet Scripture clearly says that when we serve any of these needy people, we are serving God. And the call to the prison mission fields is both a challenge and a promise to those who heed it.

Women behind bars are not only prisoners, they are also the spiritually hungry, thirsty, and sick.

Value of prison ministry

Caring changes prisoners' lives

Chaplain Judy Remley ministers to women in a Florida county jail. "You have no idea what a difference a caring person makes in the life of a prisoner," Remley says. "Women prisoners need emotional security. They need to know that someone cares about them. If they get the emotional support they long for, they are strengthened in many ways. People who write them letters, send them cards, or come just to visit, minister as surely to these prisoners as those who are professionals giving Bible studies.

"I as chaplain also appreciate those who come to serve the prisoners," Remley says. "I have a couple of people who just visit one-to-one with some of the women in jail here, and their visits lessen my burden. Their one-to-one visits are very significant. Even though they can't do everything the prisoners want them to, the personal caring shown by regular visits helps tremendously."

Remley says that jail ministries differ from prison ministries because inmates are in and out of the county jail more quickly than the prison. "They are more distracted by their upcoming court case," she said. "It's hard to help them settle into a consistent Bible study program because of that."

Study documents lasting impact

In 1990 the late Associated Press religion writer George Cornell reported on a study of the impact of religious instruction on prisoners' lives.

The study involved 190 inmates, both men and women, who between 1975 and 1979 had taken part in Christian discipleship training inside the prison and a similar number who did not take the training. The groups were matched by age, race, gender, and other factors.

Both groups had been released from prison eight to 14 years prior to the study.

Cornell's article in *The Wilson Daily Times*, of Raleigh, North Carolina, December 1, 1990, reported that those who had been involved with Christian discipleship training had an 11 percent lower rate of recidivism (return to crime) than the control group.

The recidivism rate for women prisoners who took part in the religious training was even lower—only 19 percent, compared to 47 percent among the control group of women. Although more studies are being conducted on the influence of religion on recidivism, this particular study suggests that prison ministries can have a lasting effect on the lives of prisoners.

Jails and prisons are filled with those who, having broken the law, are often themselves broken by their experiences and their behavior. Prison ministry leaders can find many ways to help. In the process, they find their own lives enriched and their faith deepened.

Chapter One

Context of Prison Ministry

Ministry performed on behalf of women in prison is the focus of this book. But each type of ministry can be understood only when we understand the life of the woman in prison, who she is, and who it is that ministers to her.

Imagine life behind bars

What would it be like to wake up every day in a cage? To be shocked from sleep by an ear-shattering buzzer? To open your eyes in an 8-by-12-foot cage made of bars and cement, furnished with two bunks, a toilet, a sink, and three shelves? No walls for privacy, just a cage surrounded by other cages to which someone else holds the key.

No morning juice with your favorite newspaper, no scrambled eggs and toast with the kids, no walking the dog or feeding the cat, no long hot shower in which to plan the day. No mirror, no closet, no window, no door, and no comfortable chair in which to relax. Just the metallic clang as prison doors snap open and you walk in a closely guarded single-file line to the cafeteria. The sounds of voices bouncing off hard cement walls and tile floors, the chill of handcuffs and chains, the boredom of prison garb.

Going to jail or prison is like entering an alien world. There is no longer a living room, dining room, kitchen, bathroom, or bedroom. The inmate can't open her refrigerator and make herself a sandwich. She can't climb into her car and drive to the store or the school or the library. She can't enjoy the pleasure of folding fresh laundry for the family or preparing her children's favorite meal.

She can't decide when to turn the light off and go to sleep or when to set the alarm to wake up in the morning.

She has no control over her space, her time, her meals, or her roommate. She has no privacy for herself, and no escape from the others sharing her incarceration.

Tens of thousands of women live behind bars in this country, and their numbers are growing daily.

According to the National Women's Law Center, in Washington, D.C., women represent the fastest-growing prison population. Between 1980 and 1993 the number of female prisoners increased approximately 313 percent.

Because there are fewer prison facilities for women, an incarcerated woman is usually much farther from her home and family than is the average male prisoner.

Picture the women inside prison

The vast majority of women prisoners are poor. Most were unemployed before being incarcerated.
Black women comprise 46 percent of the population nationwide, white women 36 percent, and Hispanic women 14 percent.

In addition to being poor, most women prisoners are also mothers. A 1994 nationwide study for the U.S. Department of Justice Bureau of Justice Statistics found that two-thirds of the nearly 39,000 incarcerated women in state prisons had at least one child younger than 18. Altogether, these women prisoners were mothers to more than 56,000 minor children. Six percent of women are pregnant when they enter prison.

Women prisoners deal with depression, guilt, and self-contempt, as a 1992 Rutgers University study found.

Carrying poor pictures of self

Bari Mitchell, a volunteer chaplain who has served women prisoners in Oregon since 1981, points out, "Success for incarcerated women is rare for a number of reasons. One is that these women's self-concept is very low. Most are prostitutes and have been misused by men and addicted to drugs from a young age."

Bringing a history of crime

Drug offenses account for more than half of the growth in the female prisoner populations in state prisons, as the 1994 Bureau of Justice Statistics study found. Nearly one in three female inmates was serving a drug offense sentence in 1991. In 1986 that number was one in eight. This increase in drug offense sentences accounted for 55 percent of the increase in the female prison population between 1986 and 1991.

Violent offenses account for 20 percent of the growth in female prisoner populations. Murder accounted for just over a third of the women sentenced for a violent offense. Women in prison for homicide were almost twice as likely to have killed an intimate (husband, ex-husband, or boyfriend) than a relative such as a parent or sibling.

Fraud, including forgery and embezzlement, are the crimes of 10 percent of the women in prison.

About 71 percent of all state female prisoners had been behind bars before, including 20 percent who had served sentences as juveniles.

Abusing substances

Almost half of the women in state prisons reported committing their crimes under the influence of drugs or alcohol.

More than half had used drugs in the month before the

current offense. About two-fifths had used drugs daily.

The percentage of women using cocaine or crack in the month before their offense increased from 23 percent in 1986 to 36 percent in 1991.

Knowing abuse from others

Women prisoners report significant histories of sexual and physical violence. The 1999 U.S. Bureau of Justice Statistics indicated that more than a third of the women in state prisons and jails reported being physically or sexually abused before they were 18 years old.

It further indicated that the women behind bars in this country do not like or respect themselves. They have been both abused and abusers. They feel guilty for the things they've done and for getting caught and sent to jail. They are mothers who cannot care for their children. They are alcoholics and drug addicts whose lives are out of their control.

Many of them are con artists, willing to say anything to get what they want. Many are depressed and angry enough to kill themselves or someone else.

Attracting Jesus' special care

These are not the kinds of people most of us would choose for neighbors or friends. Yet they are precisely the kinds of people Jesus included in His circle. They are the kinds of people He served with loving kindness, the kind of people He ate with, accepted favors from, and invited to be with Him. In fact, in Matthew 25:40, He likened Himself to people like these.

Picture the visitors who minister

Those who feel the call to help women in jails and prisons come from a variety of backgrounds and all walks of life. Whether they are college students, mid-career adults, stay-at-home moms, or retirees, they see the jail and prison cells of America as spiritual wheat fields ready for the harvest.

Some Christians write letters to prisoners. Some help prisoners continue their education even while they serve their sentences behind bars. Some provide job training.

Some embrace a ministry as simple as supplying toiletries once a month to the local women's prison or county jail, providing transportation to and from jail for children, friends, and relatives of the incarcerated woman, or visiting regularly with women behind bars. Several groups around the country bring tape recorders and children's books to mothers behind bars so that their children back home can hear "Mommy" read them a bedtime story and say, "I love you, honey."

The opportunities for service within women's jails and prisons are varied. Many times the only limitations are the imaginations of those who would minister.

CHAPTER TWO

Varieties of Ministries

> Let mutual love continue. Do not neglect to show hospitality to strangers, for by doing that, some have entertained angels without knowing it. Remember those who are in prison, as though you were in prison with them; those who are being tortured, as though your yourselves were being tortured. Do not neglect to do good and share what you have, for such sacrifices are pleasing to God. — Hebrews 13:1-3, 16, NRSV

A chaplain's priorities for ministry

Harold Allison, divisional director of chaplaincy services for Region 4 of the Florida Department of Corrections, is responsible for 13 prisons employing 21 chaplains. Two of the prisons—Broward Correctional and Dade Correctional—are only for females and house more than 1,100 women.

Asked what kinds of ministries really serve women inmates, he said, "Any type of worship service, Alcoholics Anonymous and Narcotics Anonymous, and parenting programs. These are the basic and best programs that come into the prisons.

"However, everyone does church services. It is very hard to find groups willing to do something other than a church service, and yet there are so many needs that should be addressed beyond these basic ministries."

Chaplain Allison listed these common needs for women in prison:

Transportation

"Most inmates are poor, and the women are a long way away from their homes and families. A local church could advertise a monthly van run to the prison. They could let family and friends know that on such and such a date the van will be leaving from such and such a location. And they could drive people to and from the prison. That is a very good ministry, and it helps friends and family stay connected," Allison said.

Toiletries

"Women's prisons are notoriously short of toiletries. Inmates can buy soap or deodorant in the prison canteens, but about 10 percent of the population doesn't have the money to purchase the items. Local church groups who may not want to go into the prisons personally could buy supplies such as makeup, shampoo, hand cream, soap powder, bars of soap, toothpaste, deodorant, and lotion and bring them to the prison or jail. We'll then put together a package for each prisoner, making sure that every woman has at least the basics. It's always helpful if there is some lipstick or something to help them feel feminine."

Literacy tutoring

"It is hard to find volunteers willing to teach prisoners how to read or to help them with their education. We are always looking for proctors who will help the prisoner take classes and tests, usually at the college or university level. This is a wonderful service, but not one that many people think of."

Life skills training

"Prisoners need a variety of what would be called life

skills training—such things as how to draw up a budget, how to look for a job, how to write a résumé, how to interview for a job, and how to handle money. Most of the things we take for granted are new or unknown to these women."

Childcare

"We have visiting days where spouses and children can come and stay all day. It would be a great ministry if we had older community members who would come on those days and entertain the children while the wife and husband are visiting. Such a ministry would help relieve the officers. We're always short of officers. The volunteers could act as surrogate grandparents, helping monitor the kids, reading them stories, playing with them."

Music

"To be truthful, most jails and prisons really need people willing to provide church music regularly, people who can play the piano and the organ and lead choirs," he said. "This would be such a helpful ministry to most institutions, and would be greatly appreciated from the warden on down."

Allison said that most prison officials and chaplains are open to programs that serve real needs and that help support the family unit.

In the following chapters, you will find specific helpful information on practical ministries, spiritual and religious ministries, multiple-service ministries, and ministries for the children and families of prisoners.

Section 2:

Choosing Your Emphasis

CHAPTER THREE

Practical Ministries

When people hear the term "prison ministry," they usually think of religious services such as Bible studies, prayer groups, church services, and other somewhat traditional worship meetings.

Although such religious services are often standard within jails (where individuals stay temporarily) and prisons (where individuals fulfill long-term sentences), there are many other ways to minister to women behind bars and to their families.

Since not all of us feel confident preaching or leading a song service, or even praying out loud, this chapter on ministries to women in prison will suggest many less-formal methods for service and ministry.

Quilting as art and service

The Patches & Stitches of Love Quilting Guild teaches prisoners at state and county facilities to create beautiful works of art (quilts). The quilts are donated to babies who are very ill, babies with AIDS, or to battered women's shelters.

Quilting is therapeutic for the women inmates as they express themselves through the art. Accomplishing this large task for someone else creates a sense of being needed.

Patches & Stitches teaches meaningful values and how to make a loving difference in today's world with yesterday's traditions.

For more information:

Patches and Stitches of Love
6776 Church Road
Felton, PA 17322
(717) 933-5576

Promoting abstinence: Alcoholics Anonymous

Holding AA meetings: Sarah Luke's story

Sarah Luke of Acworth, Georgia, has been conducting weekly Alcoholics Anonymous meetings for women in Cobb County Jail since 1995. She has also trained prison ministers throughout the U.S. and Russia.

"The reason I'm so interested in helping the hurting women in jail is that I hurt for most of my life," she said. "I drank to dull the pain. Most of the women in jail are there because of drug and alcohol addiction that grows out of family situations such as incest and violence—both physical and psychological violence."

Sarah, who is a member of the Marietta, Georgia, Seventh-day Adventist Church, jokes that as an only child she grew up knowing she was her mother's least favorite child.

"My mother was 17 when I was born. She gave me to a couple to raise until I was 4. Then she put me with my maternal grandma. My grandma's favorite son, my uncle, molested me when I was about 5."

When Sarah was 7, her mother remarried. "Mom and her new husband would take me to town on Saturday and drop me off with a dollar or two. I'd spend the day going to the movies. I always bought a hotdog for lunch. They'd pick me up in the evening.

"My step dad molested me when I was between the ages of 8 and 13. My mother routinely told me I was ugly, dumb, and would never amount to anything. I felt deep shame and guilt.

"I got pregnant on purpose at 16 so I could leave home," she said. Unfortunately, her husband was an alcoholic with a temper. He often hit her. Sarah turned to drink. "When I drank I didn't feel so ugly or like such a bad person," she said.

Sarah Luke had four children in short order and drank until she became an alcoholic in her late 30's. She began suffering blackouts and was deeply depressed because of her drinking. She thought of suicide many times. "I didn't really want to die, just get out of the pain," she said.

One night when Sarah was drinking heavily and very depressed, she pulled a handgun out from between her mattress and springs. "Someone gave it to me years before. I got it out that night, and I remember putting it to my mouth, then putting it up by my temple. I kept trying to think of a way to kill myself that would work, because I didn't want to become an invalid for my children, who were still living at home with me.

"I remember messing around, squeezing the trigger, and thinking This gun is probably so old it won't work anyway, when all of a sudden the gun went off and the bullet went through my arm. It bit a hole out of the bone. Let me tell you, that kind of pain sobers you up in a hurry.

"I called a friend of mine and said, 'You're not going to believe what I've just done.' The next thing I remember, my friend was there, an ambulance was there, and my friend took the children home with her. I went to the hospital, where they repaired my arm and kept me under observation for a week." Sarah carries the scar to this day. Her right arm has a deep dimple where the bullet tore through the bone and flesh.

About four years after that suicide attempt, she met Emmett Luke of Marietta, Georgia. He was attending a Seventh-day Adventist church where she'd been going. The two of them were married in 1980, about five years after they met.

"I went into a Christian treatment center for a month in August 1988, and on August 10, I knelt and accepted Jesus into my heart. I just knew I'd never have to drink again," she said. "I'd been a Baptist, a Methodist, and for 16 years I'd been a Seventh-day Adventist, but I only became a Christian on August 10, 1988. And that is when the Lord took my life and turned it around. That's when I stopped drinking."

Today the life that was so filled with pain that she had tried to end it is a blessing to others. Since 1988, Sarah has been a weekly regular at Alcoholics Anonymous.

Emmett had kidney problems, and Sarah often accompanied him to Emory University Hospital for treatments. One day as she was checking Emmett into the hospital, a woman who was being brought into detox was lying on a nearby stretcher drunk and sick. But she roused herself, reached out, and touched Sarah Luke's hair.

"That touch just changed my life," Sarah says. "I looked at that woman and said, 'I've been where you are. God loves you, and so do I.' And I gave her my card with my phone number on it."

That was the beginning of a very personal ministry aimed at helping alcoholics gain freedom from the bottle "Reaching out and helping others keeps my cup full," she said. "Helping others helps me."

When Sarah lost her husband to heart disease in 1996, she said it was a reminder that "Joy is not the absence of sorrow, but the presence of God."

"I attend regular AA meetings, and at one of them, I heard about the need in jails for AA meetings, and I volunteered to help out. I began holding AA meetings at Cobb County once a week. Now I am the coordinator, and train others. I still hold meetings, but so do others who I have trained.

"If you can meet people at their point of need, dry their tears, let them know you care, you can minister," she said. "Kind of like that old quote, 'Nobody cares how much you know until they know how much you care.'"

Starting an AA program

Complete materials on starting an Alcoholics Anonymous group in a prison or jail are available from:

General Service Office of Alcoholics Anonymous
P.O. Box 459
Grand Central Station
New York, New York 10163

As with all prison ministries, an Alcoholics Anonymous group starts with the permission and cooperation of the officials at an institution.

If the local jail or prison does not have an AA group already meeting, it will be necessary to write a proposal and follow it with a face-to-face meeting with the chaplain or top administrator of the institution. At the meeting, it can be explained how AA groups operate in other institutions and how such a group can assist inmates at release by helping them find a welcoming transition through AA groups on the outside.

It is also important to point out that AA can help the alcoholic inmate live a sober and contented life both in prison and after release.

Since AA's goal is sobriety and the only requirement for membership is a desire to stop drinking, only AA members can conduct AA meetings.

Following AA's Twelve Steps

The 12 steps of Alcoholic Anonymous, copyrighted by Alcoholics Anonymous World Services, Inc., reflect biblical principles:

1. We admitted we were powerless over alcohol—that our lives had become unmanageable.
2. We came to believe that a Power greater than ourselves could restore us to sanity.
3. We made a decision to turn our will and our lives over to the care of God, as we understood God.
4. We made a searching and fearless moral inventory of ourselves.
5. We admitted to God, to ourselves, and to another human being the exact nature of our wrongs.
6. We were entirely ready to have God remove all these defects of character.
7. We humbly asked God to remove our shortcomings.
8. We made a list of all persons we had harmed, and became willing to make amends to them all.
9. We made direct amends to such people wherever possible, except when to do so would injure them or others.
10. We continued to take personal inventory and when we were wrong promptly admitted it.
11. We sought through prayer and meditation to improve our conscious contact with God, as we understood Him, praying only for knowledge of God's will for us and for the power to carry that out.
12. Having had a spiritual awakening as the result of these steps, we tried to carry this message to alcoholics, and to practice these principles in all our affairs.

Writing letters

Edith Cooper's story of letter-writing ministry

Edith Cooper of Lookout Mountain, Georgia, was drawn into a ministry for women behind bars because of a friend's daughter.

"I helped a friend adopt a baby, and when that little baby grew up she became an alcoholic. She's a sweet girl but suffers from bulimia and alcoholism, and wound up in jail.

"Because I cared about her, I started writing to her and sending her beautiful pictures of flowers or birds that I cut out of magazines or off calendars. And I'd send her encouraging poems or articles. When the other prisoners saw her getting all this mail with all the pretty pictures, they wanted to be included."

Edith decided to make Bible studies for the other women in prison who wanted to correspond with her.

"Since I'm 83 and don't have the energy I used to have, I do everything by correspondence. I designed Bible studies to answer the questions: Who am I? Who is Jesus? Who is God? I send lessons to three girls in the prison. One is accused of killing her father, one is in for child abuse, and the third was a prostitute. I send them beautiful pictures of birds and flowers and animals. They love the pictures because the jails are so ugly. And all the girls are eager to know Jesus."

Edith has designed her Bible lessons with before-and-after questions. There is a section for the women to write down their "ideas before reading the text," and then at the end of the Bible study there is a section to write down their "ideas after reading the text."

"I comment on everything they say. I write, 'I like what you said about …' and try to comment on the best of what they say, try to bring out the best in them. In addition to the comments on the Bible studies, I write each of them a letter.

"This is a lot of work, but very rewarding. I estimate I spend six hours a week for the three girls.

"The key to this whole thing is loving these people whom you don't know. I send them inspirational stories with my letters. I want to take them out of the jail life, if only for the few minutes they are reading my letters or doing the Bible studies." Edith Cooper's letter-writing ministry is deeply personal and satisfying.

Someone Cares Prison Ministry

There are many others, like Edith, who write to inmates. There are also organized letter-writing ministries. One of them is organized by Someone Cares Prison Ministry.

Someone Cares Prison Ministry, a nonprofit faith ministry reaching out to inmates through totally risk-free letter correspondence, is operated by Don and Yvonne McClure.

"We have a blind post office box, so that letter writers never give out their own address," Don McClure said. "We've had this ministry for almost 20 years. We've had 180,000 inmates complete Adventist Bible studies and have never had a problem."

For more information:

Someone Cares Prison Ministry
P.O. Box B
Ivanhoe, CA 93235
(559) 739-7400.
sdapm@Someonecares.org
www.someonecares.org

Suggestions for writing to inmates

Whether or not you contact Someone Cares, here are 21 suggestions for writing to inmates based on those developed by the Georgia-Cumberland Conference of Seventh-day Adventists. Consider them carefully, as they can help you decide if this is a ministry you wish to pursue.

1. Prayer is essential in any endeavor for God. Pray not only for wisdom and discernment, but for your pen friends as well.
2. Use an index card to keep track of each pen friend. Record on it when you write and when the pen friend writes back. Jot down any information pertinent to your pen friend.
3. Avoid prying about their incarceration. If they volunteer information, you may feel that trust has begun to be developed. Do ask questions about prison and prison life so that you can better understand.
4. Don't write preachy letters. Attempt to develop a friendship. Do not write about your problems. Prisoners have enough problems of their own.
5. Topics of interest include current events, church events, and family events.
6. Try to be positive but honest in your writing. Share personal testimonies of what Jesus has done and is doing in your life.
7. Share funny stories or cartoons with your pen friend.
8. Share Bible promises.
9. Be regular and dependable in your writing. Make it a practice to write once a month even if you don't receive a response, just to let your pen friend know you are thinking of her. (Your pen friend may not have a stamp, pen, paper, or an envelope with which to respond to your letters.)
10. Don't make promises unless you're certain you can keep them. If your pen friend asks you to do something you

can't, be open and explain why you aren't able to comply. If she asks questions that make you uncomfortable, explain that the question is personal and you do not wish to answer.

11. When a friendship develops, you might want to recommend a Bible study course that she has not yet taken.
12. Sometimes inmates get transferred or paroled without warning. If this happens, the prison will usually return your letter rather than forwarding it.
13. You may send self-addressed envelopes with imprinted stamps if you wish (the kind you can buy at the post office), since many inmates cannot afford stamps. Do not, however, send stamps or envelopes with adhesive stamps on them. Most prisons do not allow these.
14. Prison officials must approve all items sent to inmates. Check with your pen friend to secure a list of what is allowed. Always make sure your package has been approved. Every prison has different rules regarding items that can be sent to prisoners. If your package is not approved, your pen friend will not get it and it will not be returned to you.
15. If you want to send your friend a little gift for her birthday or for Christmas, a small money order is often allowed. However, cash and checks are never allowed.
16. It is best to maintain some anonymity as a precaution. Usually pen friends do this by using only their first name and by not revealing a home address or telephone number. They might arrange to use a post office address or a church address.
17. If your name is listed in the phone book along with your address, request the phone company to remove your address.
18. It is also best to use a post office box rather than a home address for jail or prison correspondence. If it is difficult

for you to obtain a P.O. box, you may wish to have the mail go through your local church.

19. Caution: Refrain from using words such as "dear" and "love." Inmates are usually very lonely people who can easily read the wrong meaning into your words. Cross-gender letters run the largest risk of misinterpretation, so this is an area where great caution should be used. Make sure your pen friend understands from the beginning that you are corresponding only for Christian encouragement. If it become clear that the inmate has misinterpreted your intentions, it is usually best to discontinue the correspondence.
20. Anything you send to your pen friend must have her prisoner number on it or it will not get through to her.
21. Your friend may ask for your phone number. It is strongly suggested that you do not give your personal or business phone numbers. There are several reasons for this: Your phone number makes you easy to locate once the prisoner is out of prison. Your phone number could get into the hands of others within the prison who are not your friends. Phone calls from inmates are usually collect and frequent, since prison is a very lonely place.

Preparing prisoners for life outside

Creating SEED ministry: Donna Hubbard-Spearman's story

Donna Hubbard-Spearman, executive director of Revelation SEED Workshop, Inc., has worked to develop transitional housing, along with other programs designed to help incarcerated and formerly incarcerated women.

"Our mission is to assist these women in regaining their lives, families, and dignity," Donna said. "Our desire is that God will use our testimonies, our experiences, and our expertise to encourage women to be survivors, not victims. We are living testimonies, saved in the fire, not from the fire. We pray that the lives of women will be touched by the power of the living God and changed forever."

Donna and the women working with her on behalf of prisoners and their families were themselves behind bars at one time. "I served six years and eight months of a 24-year sentence for drug conspiracy," said Donna. "I spent three years in federal maximum security in Lexington, then the rest of my time in Alderson federal prison camp.

"Because of my own experience and what I went through, I know what women prisoners need.

"My first challenge in jail was the adjustment of being separated from my children. Then later, when I faced leaving prison, I had great anxiety about my release. Could I make it on the outside? Could I find a job? Could I care for my children?

"The ministry of Revelation SEED Workshop grew slowly over time—one step, one idea perpetuated another. It all began with small things—such as forming a support group outside the jail.

"Finally we realized that without stable housing, a released prisoner cannot get a job, maintain contact with her children, nor stay away from drugs and alcohol. So developing a transition center was our next step."

Today, Revelation SEED Workshop works inside the prison to help inmates begin to prepare for release. "In jail, we help them adjust to being separated from their children. Through workshops, we help them learn to end their risky behavior. Women prisoners are dealing with guilt, shame, rejection, and denial along with separation anxiety. Our classes help them learn ways to deal constructively with all these issues," Donna said.

Donna, 43, relies on Pastor Alonzo Terry, of the Solid

Rock Pentecostal Church in Atlanta, and Pastor Betty Oats, of Tampa, Florida, for support.

A wife and mother of seven, Donna says a transition center is often the missing link between a woman's incarceration and her reunification with her family.

"When you've been in prison for four years and suddenly you're out, life can become overwhelming—you have children you must care for, you've got to get a job, you've got to meet parole requirements. The stress can push you right back to the behavior that put you behind bars in the first place."

Revelation SEED Workshop's transition center offers released women a stable home. Three months before release, the prisoner is interviewed, and, if chosen, is provided with the clothing she will need on the outside. She is also provided with a support group.

A Revelation SEED Workshop mentor meets the released prisoner at the bus station and accompanies her to the transition center, where the released prisoner can stay for up to six months.

The transition center (which has room for eight women at a time) provides computer training, an employment readiness course, a substance abuse program, and classes in anger management, conflict resolution, relationship building, health care and nutrition, as well as HIV-AIDS prevention classes. If the released woman has a history of drug or alcohol abuse, she is required to attend substance abuse classes five days a week.

The transition center program designates Saturday as family day. From noon to 8:00 p.m., families visit and enjoy activities such as field trips, baking cookies together, and other family activities.

"We are a faith-based program because we know, as formerly incarcerated women ourselves, that only with the help of God and caring friends can we regain our human dignity," Donna says. "What makes us different from other ministries or transition centers is that when the women come in our door, they are face-to-face with one of their peers. Not a parole officer, but a woman who was in prison and is now leading a successful life. We try to provide everything they will need. We believe they have the ability to regain their lives, families, and dignity. We set the example ourselves."

Donna notes that the women in the transition center eat one meal a day together. This shared meal and the Saturday family days are important in facilitating the move back to normal family life, to becoming a mother again, she said.

In addition to its prison ministry and transition center, Revelation SEED Workshop has published My Mother's House, a coloring book filled with illustrations by incarcerated women, designed to help children adjust to separation from their mothers.

Donna, her two staff members, and an advisory council of 10 were all formerly incarcerated. "This is not only an important ministry for women prisoners and their families," she said, "but it is something that formerly incarcerated women all over the country can do to help others. It helps women in county jail or maximum security facilities to gain a foothold of dignity and begin the journey back into the mainstream.

Steps to a successful transition ministry

According to Donna Hubbard-Spearman, executive director of Revelation SEED Workshop, Inc., there are three basic steps to launching a successful transition ministry for prisoners and their families:

1. Identify what services you want to provide for the women and stick with those. "The reality is that you can't

help every woman with everything, so specialize," Donna said.

2. Build on community resources. "You can't do it all by yourself, so you need to develop a community support system. Form partnerships with churches, local government, or non-profit organizations that can or do serve the women you will be serving. Work with the corrections institutions in the area and women's organizations whose goals connect with yours," Donna said. "You want to develop mutual support toward meeting the needs of the incarcerated woman and her family."
3. Be prepared to make sacrifices. This kind of ministry often turns out to be a full-time commitment. Solicit and train volunteers who can help spread out the workload so that you do not become overwhelmed.

For more information, contact:

Revelation SEED Workshop, Inc.
P.O. Box 56623
Atlanta, GA 30343
(770) 961-7182

Mentoring women during re-entry: Project COPE

Based in St. Louis, Missouri, Project COPE (Congregation/Offender Partnership Enterprise) uses volunteers from local congregations to provide support for adult ex-offenders during the first year of community re-entry.

For more information:
Project COPE
3529 Marcus Ave.
St. Louis, MO 63115
(314) 389-4804

Providing skills for success: Taking Charge ministry

Taking Charge of Your Life is a program begun in 1993 by Beth Pessner at the Virginia Correctional Center for Women in Goochland, which uses volunteers to teach parenting skills and money management, including how to use credit wisely.

Prison officials credit the program's success to the fact that it is taught by volunteers from the community, whom Pessner recruits and trains.

For transition specialist Kim Hull, the critical thing is "to get human beings in contact with the offenders. The fact that someone cares enough to show up on schedule to teach, tells these offenders, 70 percent of whom were abuse victims, that they are worth something."

Learning practical money-management skills such as saving, investing, opening a checking account, and using credit wisely from local residents helps the women inmates realize they have community support.

The program is funded through a grant from AT&T given through the National Coalition for Consumer Education. For a complete description of "Taking Charge of Your life," read the article "Helping Women Break the Prison Cycle" in the Winter 1995 Virginia Tech magazine or visit the Web site: http://scholar.lib.vt.edu/ejournals/VTMAG/v17n2/page21.html

CHAPTER FOUR

Spiritual and Religious Ministries

Leading Bible studies: Bari Mitchell's story

Bari Mitchell lives and ministers in the Portland, Oregon, area. A registered nurse, Bari was a single mother with two sons when she began her jail ministry in 1981.

"One week at church a lay leader asked for someone in the congregation to write to an inmate, and I felt moved to write. So I started writing letters to a female inmate.

"Then a few weeks later the same leader asked for prayer concerning the local county jail. It seems that they were looking for someone to take Bible studies to the prisoners. I felt, or you might say, 'heard' the Lord say to me, 'go in.'

"I would never have thought of it myself. Go into the jail? It wasn't the kind of thing I would do. But I felt impressed and went to the pastor, telling him that I felt the Lord wanted me to take Bible studies to the women in jail. He said to me, 'It's a very discouraging work. Pray about it.'

"So I did. And the conviction grew that I should take up this ministry. When I told the pastor, he arranged for me to meet with the woman who had been carrying on the jail ministry work."

Bari also met with the volunteer coordinator at the local jail, and eventually, after filling out the required forms and undergoing a police check, she was cleared to enter the jail.

"The first time I walked in and heard the clang of the prison doors behind me, I thought, 'Oh, no, this is real. I'm in jail.' But I went through the experience I began to realize that these women are just like I am, only they're in trouble."

Bari observed how the woman who had been doing jail ministry interacted with the inmates, how she talked with them, how she encouraged their Bible study. Over time, Bari found herself feeling good about the project. "I went with her and sat and listened and talked. After a while I felt like, 'I'm fine here. This is not a problem, Lord.'"

Not long afterward, Bari took over the ministry completely. Today she works as a volunteer chaplain at Multnomah County Detention Center in downtown Portland, and Inverness Multnomah County Jail east of Portland. Both of these institutions house men and women.

"Success for incarcerated women is usually very low," Bari says. "Most are prostitutes and have been used by men and are addicted to drugs. Most of them started at a very young age. It is painful to see so little change in these women. They are in and out of jail often.

"Many get out and go right back to the old friends and the old ways. What is needed, I feel, is transition houses where these women can learn job and living skills and can be taken to church for fellowship."

Today Bari Mitchell has a family that depends on her. She cares for her 30-year-old son, who is handicapped, and her two grandchildren. She also has two adopted daughters, 12 and 13 years old. "Actually, I adopted them from a female inmate," she said.

"The experience of taking Bible studies into the jails has been great because it draws the inmates to me. They come up and ask why I'm there. I'm able to give them material that they want. So many of them want something to read. And so many want to read the Bible but have never learned how.

"I grade the Bible studies and ask the inmates questions about their answers. I may say, 'What do you mean by this?' and that gives us a chance to talk and learn together. I take the graded Bible studies back to them in person, and we go over everything. It has really helped me. Sometimes the women just want to talk. And so I listen with care, and that seems to be very helpful to them.

"Sometimes they'll ask my advice, and I'm able to counsel them a little. They'll ask a question and I'll say, 'Let's see what the Bible says,' and that way we can learn together from the Bible.

"Not every county jail has staff chaplains," Bari says, "but if someone feels moved by the Lord to minister, they could call the county jail and talk to the commander in charge. You just call and ask, 'How do I become a volunteer chaplain in your jail?'

"Each jail has its own requirements, so they'll guide you through."

Spiritual and religious ministries focus on building values, hope, and inner strength. While no more valuable than practical ministries, these more traditional ministries offer life-changing opportunities. The variety of spiritual and religious ministries now available demonstrates clearly that such ministry can be done in many different ways.

Conducting church behind prison walls: Jerry and Violet Miller's story

Jerry and Violet Miller, of Trion, Georgia, have been in volunteer prison ministry since 1989. They conduct church meetings in men's prisons and maintain a Bible lesson correspondence ministry with both men and women prisoners.

Members of the Summerville Seventh-day Adventist

Church, the Millers began their ministry somewhat apprehensively. "Our pastor wanted to get a ministry program going in the local prison and we thought we'd support him, but we didn't know what to expect," Vi says. "Jerry said, 'This is the Lord's work, not ours,' and so we tried to just trust in the Lord. We discovered that the chapel environment in a prison is safe. Only those prisoners who want to come to church come."

Today Jerry and Vi manage the program, training volunteers and conducting church services regularly. "Once you get a church program started, you don't want it to die," he says. "It is very hard to secure a time slot, so once you have one, you don't want to lose it."

The Millers point out that prison church services are nondenominational. "The service must encourage. It must focus on God's love and forgiveness and on the sacrifice Jesus made for each of us. And you can present stories from the Bible, but there is absolutely no proselytizing."

The Millers' church service consists of singing, praying and sharing.

"They bring their problems and their praise to church," said Vi. "It is a testimony time. Then we have a short sermon and a scripture reading."

Jerry describes some of the potential frustrations of conducting church inside a prison. "We're supposed to get an hour and a half with the inmates, but usually we only have an hour. You have to wait to be escorted in; you have to wait for the prisoners to finish their supper and be escorted into the chapel. All sorts of things nibble away at the time.

"The only thing that's consistent with a prison ministry is change. A new warden comes in, and you have to reinvent the wheel. Sometimes we find the rules changing from week to week.

"If the officers in charge feel religion is good, they'll help you in every way. If they think prisoners cannot change, they don't care about any ministry outreach."

Through their prison and correspondence ministry the Millers have learned that God can work through them.

"This ministry has taught me to depend on the Lord," Violet says. "I'm timid and shy, but I find I can stand up in front every week without fear. If the Lord can use me, He can use anyone."

Jerry says, "It's taught me that I can't solve the problems—God solves the problems. Solutions come in answers to prayer."

The Millers celebrated their 30th anniversary in 1998 and discovered that their ministry benefited from that fact. "Most of these prisoners have never seen that kind of consistency and commitment," Jerry said.

Knowing that the Millers share a long-term, committed marriage, and seeing them conduct prison church week after week, has gone a long way in developing trust among the inmates, Violet said.

"When we first started out, we spent our own money to buy literature and stamps and Bibles, but the demand and the cost grew too much for us," Violet said. "It is very important, if you're going to start this kind of ministry, that you affiliate with some larger entity to help with the expenses."

Today the Millers work with the Georgia-Cumberland Conference of Seventh-day Adventists, which supplies some of the Bible lessons and all of the postage and envelopes and enrollment cards.

The Millers continue to use their own funds for literature and Bible lessons. "Our local church helps with expenses," Vi said.

Sometimes the Millers receive requests for Bibles from

prisoners, and sometimes they receive requests from prisoners outside of Georgia. "In those cases we refer them to United Prison Ministries out of Verbena, Alabama. (The address, telephone, and Web site are listed at the end of this chapter.)

"It's important to remember that most inmates have trouble reading," Violet says. "And most of them don't use the King James Version of the Bible. What they really like is comic-book-style Bible lessons."

Cautions

The Millers caution that volunteers must be well-trained and "all on the same page." "It is important that we're all working together," Vi says.

"For a successful prison church ministry, you need reliable people. Consistency is vital to this ministry," Jerry says. "And you don't want volunteers who say anything contrary to the literature we hand out. You don't want volunteers with their own agenda, or who are overbearing. The attitude is one of loving-kindness and Christian service."

Both Vi and Jerry say it is easy to get discouraged with such a ministry.

"We pray a lot," Vi says. "We have learned not to get discouraged. When we have problems, and there are always problems, we have learned not to try and fix them, but always to pray first."

Distribution of inspirational materials

Religious books

Founded in 1981 by Richard A. Bland and his wife, United Prison Ministries International specializes in distributing Bibles, Bible lessons, and Spirit of Prophecy books to men and women behind bars.

Distributed books include The Desire of Ages, The Ministry of Healing, Christ's Object Lessons, and The Great Controversy.

For more information:

United Prison Ministries International
890 CR 93, PO Box 8
Verbena, Alabama 36091
(205) 755-4744
www.upmi.org

Christian videos

Since functional illiteracy is high in America's penal system, videos provide a vitally effective way to reach prisoners' minds and hearts.

Through Christian Videos for Prisons, thousands of videos are being placed within the hands of chaplains who specifically request them for use in their prison ministry.

The videos are provided free of charge. The ministry is evangelical and interdenominational.

For more information:

Christian Videos for Prisons
1832 S. Macdonald Suite 101
Mesa, AZ 85210-6134
1-800-332-2261
prisons@eden.org
www.christiananswers.net/prisons/home.html

Other spiritual and religious ministries

• Adventist Prison Ministry Association of the North American Division
12501 Old Columbia Pike

Silver Spring, MD 20904-6600
(301) 680-6430

Membership available. Newsletter. Yearly conventions.

• Aglow International Prison Ministry
P.O. Box 6072
Oceanside, CA 92058-6072
kjafriend@juno.com

Ministry to women prisoners through prayer and fellowship.

• Bible Believers Fellowship, Inc.
P.O. Box 0065
Baldwin, New York 11510-0065
(516) 377-0782
bbfi@prisonministry.org
www.prisonministry.org

A nonprofit nationwide Christian prison ministry that provides chaplains with free English and Spanish Christian literature and videos, including Bibles, New Testaments, Gospels of John, tracts, and the newsletter "The Good News Letter."

• Care Prison Ministries
P.O. Box 614
Trion, GA 30753-0614
(706) 734-7530

Bible studies and other literature. Prison services, newsletter.

• Florida Prison Ministries
P.O. Box 2626
Winter Park, FL 32790
(352) 728-1229

Pen pal program, visitation, services in many prisons throughout Florida, Bible correspondence studies.

• Kairos, Inc.
140 N. Orlando Ave., Suite 180
Winter Park, FL 32789-3680
(407) 629-4948
kairosnat@aol.com
www.kairosprisonministry.org

Kairos is a continuing prison ministry launched with the presentation of a three-day short course in Christianity within a correctional institution. Kairos builds strong Christian communities within the environment of correctional institutions through small, share-and-prayer groups of residents.

• Prison Fellowship Ministries
P.O. Box 17500
Washington, D.C. 20041-0500
(703) 478-0100
www.pfm.org

Founded in 1976 by former Nixon aide Chuck Colson, Prison Fellowship Ministries provides help to victims of crime, conducts in-prison and after-prison ministry, and publishes Jubilee magazine.

• Set Free Prison Ministries
P.O. Box 5440
Riverside, CA 92517
(909) 787-9907
info@prisonoutreach.org
www.prisonoutreach.org

Bible correspondence school for prison inmates.

- United Prison Ministries International

P.O. Box 8
Verbena, AL 36091
(205) 755-4744
www.upmi.org

Bibles, Bible studies, visits, training programs

Chapter Five

Multiple Service Ministries

Some ministries combine practical help and spiritual support. While ministries can flounder when people try to do too many activities, the following ministries show multi-service ministries can survive.

Carolina prison ministries: Marcia Trott's story

Marcia Trott works as a volunteer with the Carolina Conference of Seventh-day Adventists, developing programs for women inmates at Black Mountain Correctional Center. A wife and mother, Trott has worked in property management, and since 1992 has ministered to women prisoners.

"When I was in Upper Columbia Academy I heard a student mission story, and I prayed that if God would train me to be a missionary in the U.S., I'd be one. He just had to let me know," she said.

As she looked back over her life, she could see the hand of God directing events so that she can serve effectively in the mission field of women's prisons.

"There is no doubt in my mind that God has led me to this ministry," Marcia said. "Through my Bible study, through my personal friendships and my own experiences, God has given me insights and understandings that enhance the ministry program at Black Mountain."

Marcia recalled her own childhood abuse, and the compensating behaviors she has developed to deal with her dishonor. She recalled working with a dysfunctional classmate and "learning the hard way that people can pull the wool over your eyes."

"Today, I work with abused women on the outside of prison," Marcia said, "and all the experiences give me a deep inner understanding of the women in jail. I can see God's leading every step of the way.

"In our ministry at Black Mountain, we have two kinds of people: sponsors and volunteers. The volunteers receive training and go into the prison itself to conduct reading programs, abuse seminars, or stop smoking clinics."

Marcia and the volunteers conduct church services once a month. "The service is nondenominational, emphasizing God's love and forgiveness and the love of Jesus Christ," she said.

"A sponsor (every sponsor for a woman prisoner must be a woman) accompanies the prisoner she's sponsoring outside the institution," Marcia explained. "The sponsor can take a prisoner to church, on hiking trails, to town to go shopping, or to the lake. A sponsor is a friend and mentor."

Special events

Twice a year Marcia and her volunteers work with the prison programmer to create special events for the women inmates.

"In February," Marcia said, "we provide supplies so that the women can make Valentine cards for their loved ones. We bring rubber stamps and stamp pads, pencils and pens and paper so that they can fashion personal Valentines. After they've made their cards, we have a little celebration with fresh homemade bread and homemade jam. It gives a festive feeling to the event."

In June there is another special event coordinated with Marcia and her volunteers. "Most of the women prisoners have anniversaries in June," Marcia noted, "but they don't get to celebrate because they are behind bars. We go in and hold an ice cream feed that month, just a celebration with banana splits. It means a great deal to them.

"What is amazing is the amount of love that can be shown in such simple events, such ordinary things."

Cautions

Marcia Trott said that her years in prison ministry have taught her to be cautious.

"Prisoners are tremendous manipulators," she pointed out. "They will try to break the rules. They may ask you for special favors, and you must make sure that the prison allows what they are asking or you must refuse as kindly as possible. "It's also important to make sure you don't wear clothes that are the same color as the prisoners' uniforms."

For more information:

Carolina Prison Ministries
P.O. Box 2206
Fairview, NC 28730
(828) 628-4819; (828) 628-0846

Centerforce: Supporting visitors to prisons

Centerforce, based in San Quentin, California, administers a network of prison visitor centers at all California state prisons.

Established in 1971, Centerforce provides transportation between public transit and prisons, an emergency clothing exchange, information and referral, limited childcare, refreshments, and respite before and after visiting.

Centerforce also educates community groups about prison visiting and the criminal justice system on a state and national level.

For more information:

Centerforce
64 Main St.
P.O. Box 336
San Quentin, CA 94964
(415) 456-9980

You-Fed-Me, Inc.: Providing spiritual and physical food

Based in Raleigh, N.C., the interdenominational You-Fed-Me, Inc. Prison Ministries was founded in 1987 by Jerry and Karen Campbell, both ordained ministers who had served on the Governor's Resource Council for Prisons.

You-Fed-Me provides food for the body and the spirit—covered dish meals are prepared by volunteers and served after Bible study.

You-Fed-Me is active in Wake Correctional Center, Polk Youth Center, and the North Carolina Women's Correctional Institute.

In an effort to reach prisoners who are not interested in traditional religious study and fellowship, You-Fed-Me has added basketball games, drama, dance and rap music to its ministry.

For more information:

You-Fed-Me
4205 Wake Forest Road, Suite 101
Raleigh, N.C. 27609
Phone: (919) 876-7500

CHAPTER SIX

Children of Prisoners Ministries

In this chapter, you will find a variety of ministries focused on the children and families of women prisoners, ideas on developing ministry programs, and a list of resource groups and organizations that conduct prison ministries. It is in no way exhaustive but illustrates the many possibilities of "visiting" the imprisoned with loving service and restoring hope to their lives.

You may decide to affiliate with some of the programs listed, or you may want to imitate what they do while customizing your ministry to meet the needs of your own specific jail or prison.

Angel Tree: providing Christmas gifts to children

The Angel Tree program provides Christmas gifts to children of prisoners.

Usually operated through a church congregation, it is an organized program of Prison Fellowship, which keeps a computer database of prisoners with children.

Churches participating in the Angel Tree program match children in the geographical area who have parents in prison with church members who want to give those children Christmas gifts.

Information about each child is written on large, colorful tags provided by Angel Tree. The tags are hung on a Christmas tree in the church where members can choose a tag and buy the child gifts and wrap the gifts.

The goal of Angel Tree is to provide each child with two gifts—a toy and an article of clothing. The combined value is generally about $35.

Shortly before Christmas, the gifts are delivered to the child's home, usually by a team from the local church. The gifts are given in the name of the absent parent and Jesus. Age-appropriate materials donated by the American Bible Society are available to help gift deliverers make a gospel presentation to each child. There are also special materials to help a gift deliverer tell the Christmas story to an Angel Tree child.

Some churches hold a party and distribute the gifts during the party. In that way they bring the children to church and begin to build personal bonds between the church and the prisoners' families.

The Angel Tree Web site says: "Angel Tree is for all kinds of churches—large and small. Some churches can sponsor a few children; others can sponsor many. Whether your church is large or small, Angel Tree can bring a great blessing to you and to any number of families to which you minister."

For more information:

Central California Prison Fellowship
438 East Shaw Ave. PMB #231
Fresno, CA 93710-7654
(559) 224-8020

Angel Tree
P.O. Box 17500
Washington, DC 20041-6069
(703) 478-0100, ext. 557
www.angeltree.org

Family Matters: giving support to mothers and children

A program of The Parent Center in Little Rock, Arkansas, Family Matters focuses on children of female offenders and the relatives who care for them.

Family Matters provides crisis intervention for children following the arrest of their mother. It provides family life education groups for mothers in jail, assistance planning for the care of children of incarcerated women, support groups and parent education for grandparents and other relatives, and other assistance.

For more information:

Family Matters
The Parent Center
5905 Forest Place, Suite 205
Little Rock, AR 72207
(501) 666-6833

Girl Scouts Beyond Bars: keeping daughters in touch

This national program aims to keep mothers and daughters in touch through Girl Scouting.

A local group of volunteers who are Girl Scout leaders or who know about Girl Scouts works with the jail or prison to establish a Girl Scout troop that includes the incarcerated mothers and their daughters.

The weekly or monthly Girl Scout meetings inside the jail or prison help to keep the mother-daughter connection alive.

The Girl Scout volunteers serve as role models not only for the daughters but also for the incarcerated mothers.

This program is costly in terms of time and money. It is working with a high-risk population—girls who have seen and experienced more than most people have, and girls who are so geared to being disappointed that it is difficult to develop trust. The commitment level for volunteers in Girl Scouts Beyond Bars is high, but the rewards can be great.

For more information contact Girl Scouts of U.S.A., 1-800-478-7248, or call your local Girl Scout Council.

Hour Children, Inc.: providing foster care

Hour Children, Inc., provides foster care for children of incarcerated women. The program works with incarcerated mothers and their children to strengthen family ties through advocacy, visiting assistance, and social services.

For more information:

Hour Children, Inc.
36-11A 12 Street
Long Island City, New York 11106
(718) 433-4724

Incarcerated Mothers Program: providing educations to mothers

Based in New York City, Incarcerated Mothers Program/Edwin Gould Service for Children provides home visits to children of incarcerated women, teaches parenting skills, provides HIV/AIDS support, and more.

For more information:

Edwin Gould Service for Children
104 E. 107th Street
New York, NY 10029
(212) 410-4200

Kids Need Moms: strengthening a sense of parental responsibility

Developed by the Florence Crane Women's Correctional

Facility in Coldwater, Michigan, Kids Need Moms is a multidimensional program helping incarcerated mothers maintain their parental responsibilities, and helping children of prison mothers feel that they still have a mom.

Kids Need Moms includes child development classes, family counseling, and structured visits.

Since a lack of transportation is one major reason children are often unable to visit their mothers in prison, Kids Need Moms is developing a system of monthly visitation, with volunteer drivers supplying transportation to and from the facility.

Obtaining contributions of volunteer time, children's toys and games, appropriate furnishings for the playroom, and money is an ongoing effort to maintain Kids Need Moms. Forming congenial rapport with local businesses, citizens, large companies, and other interested groups helps provide for this quality program that insures healthy family bonding.

For more information:

Kids Need Moms Coordinator
Florence Crane Women's Facility
38 Fourth St.
Coldwater, MI 49036
(517) 279-9165, ext. 1402

MIWATCH: transporting children to visit mothers

Based in Little Rock, Arkansas, MIWATCH (Ministries to Incarcerated Women and Their Children) pairs children of inmates with screened volunteers to transport them to and from prison for visits with their mothers. The program also collects personal hygiene items for the inmates.

For more information:

MIWATCH
2224 Main St.
Little Rock, AR 72206
(501) 372-5113

S.K.I.P., INC.: developing children's skills

S.K.I.P. (Save Kids of Incarcerated Parents) is a network of services for children (from one month to 18 years of age) of incarcerated parents. The services include educational enrichment, character and career development, "Kids Helping Kids" peer mentoring, SKIP volunteers, and counseling services.

The educational and enrichment program teaches basic verbal and writing skills, problem-solving skills, creative arts, and family-life skills. Using the local library, this program also helps children learn research and reference skills.

"Kids Helping Kids" works with high school student mentors who are trained how to work with children of incarcerated parents. Children of inmates feel less conspicuous and self-conscious, knowing that they have peer support.

For more information:

SKIP Inc.
Community Resource Services
669 Bush Drive
Hope Hull, AL 36043
(334) 284-8103
skipinc@mindspring.com

The Storybook Project: recording mothers' voices

This ministry is both simple and profound. A few volunteers with limited resources can bring this ministry to jail or prison inmates.

A variety of new children's books and 60-minute audiotapes are taken into the prison. Volunteers help the incarcerated mothers choose an appropriate book and read it onto the tape, along with a short and loving message to their child.

The tape and the book are then mailed to their child or children.

This project can be done at special times of the year such as Christmas or Mother's Day, or it can be part of a parenting or literacy program.

The child receiving the tape can play it again and again, listening to mother's voice reading and saying, "I miss you, honey, and I love you."

For a detailed description of how to get started, how to obtain needed supplies, and how to work with the prisoner to make a great tape, go to the web site: www.elca.org/wo/storybk.html

Women's Prison Association and Home, Inc.: offering support to parents

Based in New York City, Women's Prison Association and Home, Inc., provides parent training, counseling, living skills, education, employment assistance, and more. It also has publications that may be of use in smaller prison ministries. Among the publications available are Breaking the Cycle of Despair, and Don't Forget About Your Children.

For more information:

Women's Prison Association and Home, Inc.
110 Second Avenue
New York, NY 10003
(212) 674-1163

SECTION 3:

Getting Started

CHAPTER SEVEN

Guidelines for Effectiveness

Women prisoners desperately need spiritual support and caring friends to help them through the trauma of incarceration and to help them develop or regain the strength to live productively.

Many jails and prisons also need caring volunteers to provide programs and motivation unavailable through the prison system. Although there is always a mound of paperwork, a number of meetings, and a background check of those who wish to volunteer, chaplains and others in charge of the institution often welcome well-thought-out programs of a spiritual or uplifting nature that can enrich the lives of inmates.

Beginning a prison ministry to meet the needs of women inmates requires commitment, concern for the women and their problems, the ability to work within the jail or prison system, and the ability to continue in service even when "successes" may be few.

Steps to success

Those who have spent years ministering to prisoners have developed some general and basic steps to take when considering whether to join or launch a prison ministry.

- To begin with, pray for guidance. What kind of ministry would most clearly serve the women prisoners in the local jail or prison? Listen for God's leading.
- Not every ministry is overtly religious. While church

services and Bible studies are obvious ways to minister to the spiritual needs of women inmates, God may impress you with other ways to meet inmates' needs and show loving-kindness. Remain open to the leading of God's Spirit.

- Develop a vision of what you want to do for the prisoners. What do you want to do? How will you do it? How often will you do it? How will your program benefit the prisoners? How will it benefit the jail or prison?
- Discuss your plan with your pastor, with other groups or organizations that minister in jails, and with lay leaders in your church whose insight might prove useful.
- Try to develop the interest and help of other church members by announcing your plans in church and by putting a brief paragraph about your proposed ministry in the bulletin. If church members do not feel the same call to ministry that you have felt, try to develop interest and help from other service or non-profit organizations in your town.
- Gain as much knowledge as you can about the institution you wish to visit before asking permission to provide services there.
- Write a letter/proposal, clearly stating the program you wish to start, the goals you believe it will reach, the objectives you and your church have for the program, and the reason you want to work in that particular institution. In other words, fit your ministry to the institution's (and women prisoners') needs. Send your letter/proposal to the top prison or jail administrator.
- Follow up with a phone call to that administrator and schedule an appointment to meet with him or her and discuss your proposal.
- If possible, visit an institution with an already-established

prison ministry team in order to gain some "on-the-job training" and understanding.

- Use resources that are available within your denomination and/or community. Enlist other groups and organizations so that the time and financial requirements can be shared.

Guidelines for volunteer ministry

Those who train lay volunteers for ministry say adhering to a few basic principles reduces problems and increases the chances of success.

The first principle is training. Learn from someone who has already conducted this kind of ministry. Work with someone in the kind of ministry you want to have. Jesus gave direction and supervision to the disciples. That example should guide all who set out to serve.

When ministering one-to-one in the prisons, remember that you will most likely be working with women who are different from you. In addition to their incarceration, an array of problems leaves them vulnerable and needy. They may have a lack of formal education, no job skills, addictions to drugs and alcohol, a background of abuse, and no loving family to visit them.

Those who serve people in physical, spiritual, or emotional need enter into a sacred relationship. The minister or servant stands in a position of trust.

Even though many prison inmates may not trust you, they need to know they can. They need to know that you will listen to them with a caring heart, and not interrupt to give advice. They need to know that confidential information shared with you will remain confidential. And they need to know that you are dependable and will be there when you say you will.

Volunteers in service ministry translate emotions into responsible moral behavior. Although you may feel warmly toward those you serve, they are not your friends. Friends share equally and support and care for one another. As a volunteer, you are there to serve, to offer care and support, not to receive it.

Remember to maintain boundaries (both physical and emotional) that protect you and the women you serve. Respect their privacy and personhood by never revealing information shared in confidence. Do not share more personal information about yourself than is needed. Do not tease. Do not hug. (Most jails and prisons do not allow hugging, but even if yours does allow such physical contact, you ought not to initiate it.) For your own protection, do not give personal information to the women you serve. Do not give them your home or work phone numbers or addresses. As a volunteer in service, you minister to real people, people who deserve the best you can give. You are called as a woman of faith to act in responsible, ethical ways, and to respect the inmates' boundaries, always seeking to do good and not harm.

Prison ministry do's and don'ts

Do's

1. Whether ministering in a jail or prison, obey all the rules and regulations of that particular institution.
2. When you go to the jail or prison, leave the following in your car: pocketbooks, wallets, briefcases, money, and non-essentials.
3. Always carry identification.
4. Be prepared to submit to a search at any time.
5. Keep your promises to a prisoner.
6. Always consult the institution chaplain or the leader of

your ministry group when you are in doubt.

7. Always be a Christian friend to inmates.
8. Share your faith with inmates.
9. Be dependable.
10. Be patient.
11. Be honest.
12. Be a good listener.
13. Have all books or literature that you take into the jail or prison checked by a security officer.
14. Be trustworthy when someone shares with you personal or confidential information.
15. Try to find ways to encourage and give hope. Women in prison are often suffering depression, guilt, and self-contempt. They need kindness and hope more than judgment and advice.
16. Be very kind and courteous to everyone.
17. Be natural.
18. Remember that as a prison ministry worker, you represent Jesus Christ (not yourself).

Don'ts

1. Don't give to or take anything from inmates.
2. Don't allow the inmates to become too personal with you. 3. Familiarity breeds contempt.
4. Don't give inmates your home address or phone number.
5. Don't ask why the resident is in prison.
6. Don't allow residents to "con" you with overly dramatized stories of being falsely accused, unjustly incarcerated, or inhumanely treated.
7. Don't make inflammatory statements or careless remarks to staff or residents about political groups, other religious groups, ethnic groups, individual residents, other prison ministry volunteers, or other "outside" individuals.

8. Don't assume a resident is innocent or guilty, and do not give legal counsel or advice.
9. Don't reveal personal details, if you are aware of them, about the lives of staff members, especially to prisoners.
10. Don't aid or abet the escape of a prisoner.
11. Don't take medications (legal drugs) into any institution.
12. Don't take cameras or tape recorders onto prison grounds without permission from prison officials.
13. Don't take gum into an institution, either in your mouth or on your person.
14. Don't engage in affectionate or intimate behavior with prisoners or with others in your prison ministry in front of prisoners.
15. Don't leave clothing carelessly where it may be picked up and worn by prisoners.
16. Don't park your car in other than designated parking areas.
17. Don't be shocked or surprised by anything prisoners might say or how they say it.
18. Don't deliberately try to persuade prisoners to change their religious preference.
19. Don't forget that your relationship with all prisoners should be of a professional nature.
20. Don't become involved in transacting personal business for prisoners.
21. Don't become discouraged.

The Lay Chaplain Project

Chaplain Etta C. Rossman, head chaplain of the Virginia Correctional Center for woman has recently compiled and made available a new and valuable resource, The Lay Chaplain Project. This booklet offers many helpful topics for prison ministry, such as "Listening," "Pastoral Care in Prisons,"

"Unique Experience of Grief in Prison," "Boundaries: Defining Who you Are," "How to Take Care of Yourself," "Sexual Abuse, Rape, Incest and Molesting," and "Pastoral Care to Persons Trapped in the Victim Role." These chapters offer the advice and guidelines of many prison chaplains. To receive this booklet, or for more information, call Chaplain Rossman's, or her colleague lay Chaplain Bill Bolton, at 804-784-3582, ext. 235.

CHAPTER EIGHT

Outline for Program of Dedication to Prison Ministry

by Penny Shell

A service of dedication can give important support to those who are entering prison ministry. In some cases, the service also may inspire others to be aware of their own call to this or a similar ministry. And it can educate the religious community to the importance of the ministry and suggest to them ways to be supportive. The following program, a service of dedication for those who are entering a ministry to those in prison, can be used as part of a larger church service or as a separate service. The responsive liturgy and hymn singing create strong involvement by all participants.

This model service can be used as it appears or adapted to meet the local need.

The one being dedicated to this ministry should, ahead of time, select those family and close friends who will stand with her at the time indicated.

Acknowledging God's presence

Worship leader

Let us bring our minds and hearts to quietness
as we focus on these four things:
one, the pain of imprisonment;

two, God's love for the imprisoned;
three, those who sense a called to prison ministry;
and four, ways in which we as a community of believers
can support God's work of ministry to those in prison.
Silently let us invite God's Spirit into our hearts
as we begin this dedication service.

—Silent prayer during instrumental solo for one stanza and chorus of hymn, "Breathe on Me, Breath of God"; then a song leader invites the community to sing the two stanzas below.

Hymn

Breathe on Me, Breath of God[2]
Breathe on me, Breath of God,
Fill me with life anew,
That I may love what Thou dost love,
and do what Thou wouldst do.

Breathe on me, Breath of God,
Til I am wholly Thine,
Until this earthly part of me
Glows with Thy fire divine.

Worship leader

Thank you, God, for your presence with us. Amen.

Confessing our sins

Worship leader

Let us confess our own imprisonment to sin.

Community

Living in apparent freedom, O God, we confess the times that we have been captive to evil desires and debilitating habits, the times we have been imprisoned by narrow and judgmental thoughts.

We confess the times we have distanced ourselves from those who needed us—the hungry, the thirsty, the sick, the stranger, the poor, and the imprisoned.

"If we say that we have not sinned, we make [God] a liar, and [God's] word is not in us."[3]

Forgive us, Lord.

Receiving forgiveness

Worship leader

God has promised that "if we confess our sins, [God] who is faithful and just will forgive us our sins and cleanse us from all unrighteousness."[4] If then, we say we are not forgiven, we make God a liar, and God's word is not in us.

Community

Thank you, merciful God, for forgiveness that gives us clean hearts and renewed spirits.[5]

Hymn

O Master, Let Me Walk With Thee[6]

O Master, let me walk with Thee
In lowly paths of service free;
Tell me Thy secret; help me bear
The strain of toil, the fret of care.

Help me the slow of heart to move
By some clear, winning word of love;
Teach me the wayward feet to stay,
And guide them in the homeward way.

Teach me Thy patience; still with Thee

In closer, dearer company,
In work that keeps faith sweet and strong,
In trust that triumphs over wrong;

In hope that sends a shining ray
Far down the future's broadening way;
In peace that only Thou canst give,
With Thee, O Master, let me live.

Focusing on God's love for those in prison

First reader

"When the Son of Man comes in his glory, and all the angels with him, then he will sit on the throne of his glory. All the nations will be gathered before him, and he will separate people one from another as a shepherd separates the sheep from the goats."[7]

Second reader

"Then the king will say to those at his right hand, 'Come, you that are blessed by my Father, inherit the kingdom prepared for you from the foundation of the world; for I was hungry and you gave me food, I was thirsty and you gave me something to drink, I was a stranger and you welcomed me, I was naked an you gave me clothing, I was sick and you took care of me, I was in prison and you visited me.'"[8]

Congregation

"And the king will answer them, 'Truly I tell you, just as you did it to one of the least of these who are members of my family, you did it to me.'"[9]

Hymn

Come, Ye Disconsolate[10]

Come ye disconsolate, where'er ye languish;
Come to the mercy seat, fervently kneel;
Here bring your wounded hearts, here tell your anguish;
Earth has no sorrow that heaven cannot heal.

Joy of the comfortless, light of the straying,
Hope of the penitent, fadeless and pure!
Here speaks the Comforter, tenderly saying,
"Earth has no sorrow that heaven cannot cure."
Here see the Bread of Life; see waters flowing
Forth from the throne of God, pure from above;
Come to the feast of love—come, ever knowing
Earth has no sorrow but heaven can remove.

Setting apart the one(s) called to minister to those in prison

Worship leader

This day we set aside the one(s) called to minister to those in prison and invite her (him, them) and the family members and friends that she has previously invited to come forward: [name or names of the one(s) being dedicated are read as the designated persons come to the center of the platform.]

Worship leader

Do you believe that God is calling you to minister to those in prison?

Those dedicated to prison ministry

I do (or "We do").

Worship leader

Do you as members of the community recognize God's

call upon this person [or these persons] and the gifts needed for this ministry?

Community

I do [or "We do"].

Worship leader

You who are being dedicated begin this ministry, to what do you commit yourself [yourselves]?

Those dedicated to prison ministry

Believing that God has called me to minister to those in prison, I choose to respond to this call.
I will be consistent.
I will do the best I can,
leaving the results to God.
I will look for Jesus in each prisoner, as I seek to serve.
With the guidance of the Holy Spirit,
I will seek to avoid both cynicism and gullibility.
I will seek to stay open to God's guidance and timing ready to change my methods or end my efforts.
Toward this end, I ask you, my faith community, for prayers, counsel, and material support.
I ask for your patience and encouragement.

Community

The Lord bless you and keep you.
The Lord bless those in prison through you.
The Lord guide us to support you wisely.
The Lord give you courage and wisdom and strength.
So we set you apart for this ministry.
Amen.

Supporting prison ministry

Worship leader

Let us bring a token of our support for this new ministry as the offering is collected.

—Offering for Prison Ministry is collected during the next hymn

Hymn

Take My Life and Let It Be [11]

Take my life, and let it be
Consecrated, Lord, to Thee;
Take my hands, and let them move
At the impulse of Thy love,
At the impulse of Thy love.

Take my lips, and let them be
Filled with messages from Thee;
Take my silver and my gold,
Not a mite would I withhold,
Not a mite would I withhold.

Take my love; my Lord, I pour
At Thy feet its treasure store,
Take myself, and I will be,
Ever, only, all for Thee,
Ever, only, all for Thee.

Departing to serve

Worship leader

Dismiss us, Lord, with Your blessing.
May each of us joyfully may take up the service to which You have called us and for which You have gifted us. And

if we have not yet found our own unique ministry, lead us to find it. Amen.

—Community leaves to greet those newly dedicated to service.

Endnotes

[1] New Revised Standard Vision, (Hereafter abbreviated as NRSV).

[2] "Breathe on Me, Breath of God," SDA Hymnal, No. 265, verses 1 and 3.

[3] 1 John 1:10 NRSV

[4] 1 John 1:9 NRSV.

[5] Ezekiel 36: 25 and 26.

[6] "O Master Let Me Walk with Thee, " SDA Hymnal, No. 574, all verses.

[7] Matthew 25:31-33, NRSV.

[8] Matthew 25:34-36, NRSV.

[9] Matthew 25:40, NRSV.

[10] "Come, Ye Disconsolate," SDA Hymnal, No. 477, all verses.

[11] "Take My Life and Let It Be," SDA Hymnal, No. 330, verses 1, 3, and 5.